Other poetry by Joan Retallack

Circumstantial Evidence

Errata 5uite

Icarus FFFFFalling

AFTERRIMAGES

•

JOAN RETALLACK

WESLEYAN UNIVERSITY PRESS
Published by University Press of New England
Hanover and London

Wesleyan University Press
Published by University Press of New England, Hanover, NH 03755
© 1995 by Joan Retallack
All rights reserved
Printed in the United States of America   5   4   3   2   1
CIP data appear at the end of the book

*The publisher gratefully acknowledges the support of Lannan Foundation
in the publication of this book.*

Some of the work in this volume has appeared—in present or earlier form—
in the following magazines:
*Aerial, Avec, CCLM Poetry, HOW(ever), Object, O.blēk, Painted Bride Quarterly,
Raddle Moon, So To Speak, Torque, Washington Review of the Arts.*

Icarus FFFFFalling was published as a chapbook by Leave Books, Spring 1994.

AFTERRIMAGES

ALTERRIMAGES

....

AFTERTHOUGHTS

....

AFTER/ORS

....

AFTERMATH

....

.

On July 16, 1945, as the countdown at Alamogordo approached zero the P.A. system began to broadcast music from a nearby radio station operating on the same freque ncy. This is how the explosion of the first atomic bomb came to be accompanied by a Tchaikovsky waltz.   Victor Weisskopff, Manhattan Project Physicist

Newton suffered for many years from an after-image of the sun caused by incautiously looking at it through a telescope. *Syd. Soc. Lex. s. v. 1879, OED*

We tend to think of afterimages as aberrations. In fact all images are after. That is the terror they hold for us. Genre Tallique, *Glances*

After, whistling or just_____

Anon

•

This book is dedicated to Holly Arnao Swain

and to Caitlin, Walker, and Erin

CONTENTS

AFTERRIMAGES

Afterrimages in what follows were
determined by chance procedures.

afterImage

Color Plate 25

Arising from the phenomenon of color adaptation are the effects of color contrast and the related phenomenon of afterimages. If we look steadily at a color, the eyes partly adapt to it and tend to see it as white. If we then look at another color, the condition of the eyes is such that they tend to subtract the first color from the second. That is, they tend to move the second color toward the complimentary of the first. This effect is local in the eye, so that if the first area has a strongly marked pattern, this pattern appears in the second area as an *afterimage*. See Color Plate 25.

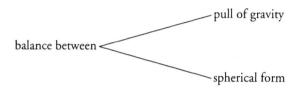

covering of short hairs or fur

something on or near the surface

i.e.specificcrystallineformoftaxonomiccategories

....

So reulith hire hir hertes gost withinne,
That though she bende, yeet she stant on roote

———————————————————

rs o

ne   th su

orm   onomi ate

.. ..

e hir hert

this was morning

deep in her body

delicious asymmetry of sight and sound

sourire jaune's yellow smile

scenes of translation

defies translation

Saph [...]gment
∪ ∪ –– –– ––   –– ––∪ ∪ ––?
(now she shines among Lyd. ..wom…………..)?

---

od

gh an

ne

e   lat

ns io

vol low on radio • in Tangier

no smoke but smell of alarm

(see a pre-Socratic on fire in the mind)

nice being out here in the sun

(or St. Augustine on time)

±o = no future tense in dreams = o±
(poetry eludes genre as well)

sage of the ectopic eye

logical series of unsolicited occasions

———————————————————

(see   i   in   e

            in   e   in

                            o

                            s w

            ec

            s

womendressedlikemenpretendingtobewomen

whtsthpntfvnshng

he said all out of proportion

not a board game

natures former artifice

perhaps the social drama analogy

HOW TO eat a _____ and stay on a diet

_____

all   of   tion

oar   gam

rm   art

garden wall battlement

YO MAMA

POMPANADA

....

random intelligence echoes planets and stars

blue spiral notebook + shiny chrome pen

=

look out /the/ window see Chaucer in /the/ angle of /the/ rain

(*The theef fil over bord al sodeynly*)

---

blu   chr m pen

(*Th*

need to give latitude which is often silence and/or

Virginia said she likes the word *breach*

whydon'tfliesdielikeflies

[........To speke of wo that is in mariage..........
Men may devyne and glosen up and doun
But wel I woot expres withoute lye]

142
.........] all this I see
..........] plainly] now

at this point Paul

mentioned that

sunbeams are

extracted from
cucumbers in
Gulliver's Travels

————————————————————————

....] all th

oint P

nb

CO...INCIDENTS

Uncle Herbie's last words: *ten o'clock*

but only one etc.

(thik'it) /ME thikket (unattested) < OE oiccet
[*thiccet, thikket*] <oicce [*thicce*] thick. tegu-.
Thick. Germanic*thiku.[Pok.*tegu-* 1057.]

n a t u r e s s o f t g e o m e t r y s t r e e s

riddle of the three sleeves

natures/rin/secycle

culturess/pin/cycle

TIGHT   LITTLE   GREY   CURLS

_____

                    cycl

               GR

we are entirely happy with our prospects
(problemoftheunreliablenarratorortwo)

rainbow colored shoelaces
thistle 'n other natural graffiti

Discipline #34

arid and semi-arid regions and remarks

sharp or poi ted objects or remarks

we are not members of the class of all
classes which can not entertain themselves

random access mem-O-rees

single engine aer-O-plane

....

when the earthquake was over
they filled a glass to the rim with water
and placed it on a table for the dead

....

ter
ead

[th] these [are] the things that made us human

S-curve   S-hook   th-

[1   1   2   3   5   8   13............

lurk   lucktool   ladle   saves

non sexist naming of hurricanes (saves)

any of various pigeon-like birds

any of various pigeon-like lurk

any of various pigeon-ladle saves

pigeon lucktool sex various nonist

Incidence:
dar muir merr-cend.....(over mad-head sea)

---

urk

on-ladle

sea

schwoop he's gone!

schwoop "he"s gone!

schwoop he's "gone"!

SMAJ

such elegiac tendencies
[*cen díl daimi risi....*
without having to pay a [rogue]
band of [rogue] story-tellers]

————————————————

ne!

S

ch
[*cen*

OMINOUS ANIMA

could be tragic if still possible

snagged mid-sentence

now no ""god" is able to restore a
"virgin" (sic) after her (sic) "downfall""

[preceding to appear illuminated in pastel colors]

{something about a nasal twang}

. . . .

snagge

        od"

                    in pastel

            twa

the box one day was brought into the house

they took his mother out in a wicker basket

someday they will take away the future tense

the preceding may be naive (U–L–G–E?)

seduction of momentum
piercing radii
desiderium oculorum

where and why does the truth lie

. . . .

                                        –G–E?)

                                        . . .

HEEREENDETHTHETALEOFTHEMANOFLAWE

of moustaches that wax and wane

(sincetheEnglishhavebeenherewehavenodreamsanymore) *Anon*

o n e l a s t e x p l o d e d v i e w

. . . .

nd

eweh

p l o d

                              everyone was puzzled how
                              11 native speakers could
                              get into so much trouble

still later Calvino's sixth memo it

still later it they it

the in in the vernacular out of inferno theory

in the late 18th century they in the Cornish language it became
        (extinct)
it could no still later it no longer could be it that it was said they
later still to get the in out of integrity it too

_____

Note: it came from Sears
no longer fulfilling requirements of harmony
measure & light
a private ratio of movements

does anyone know

which planet(s) sang soprano

over Puget sound

Z(thankgodtheyturnedthevolume)

———————————————————————

ang sopr

Lana: Please machine give piece of chow

(thanatoast)

we will be working in teams

c r e e p i n g l o g o p h i l i a

                    his posthumous grape jokes

                    her cruel but unusual

((justwhatis(was)(were)the rhetoric(s)ofdispassion))

[.........*she then*......*si*......]other fragments of uncert
ain location 37, 43 (like VII 4)(later part of III?)

───────────────────────────

           ustwhat   disp

your c u p i s l e a v i n g a r i n g o n *my* t a b l e

see RHYTHM and FORM p.5

(*Enna Labraid* etc.) quoted p.4, above,

translators note on the

fabled indifference of gods

here lies[   ]entire totem of body[   ]parts

silk pilfer nasturtium semiotic *ad sequitur*

see other *Italic Poetries* p.3

α) *Hy*ge sceal *heard*ra, *heorte* be cenre;

ß) (moping virgins [*versions*] of all genders [*genres*])

....

s[   ]ent

1. No God can be snagged in a pastel twang

this is this the famous spacetimed continuum

this page is crisp   CRISP!

"I" am afraid to fly
_____

∴ (dissyllable throughout) ∴

Terra pestem teneto : salus hic maneto.   DLHR, p.58

-charm for foot pain-

[*word foot* defined as
word containing at least
one strong (acute) stress]

[here the logic seems clear]

but
the lear in clear
the ear in lear
the a in ear
the in
the

(This is this meant to explain Ptolemy's "Handy Tables"
 with naked torsos gesticulating in little niches atop each
 column of text.)
Is *this* the anatomy of melancholy?
Does seeing imply distance?

---

text breaks into architecture of page
floating Figs
scholar riding in Capital C

St. Cuthbert *all' curyouste he refused*
curiositas (*curo*, to care), Medieval sin
this is not to imply that we are any better

off

[................*fed*..] [....*re*.......*ypi*..... ....*erg*........]

the dynamics of the picture forced him
to show roundness as a square

....

                              tect

                    Cap

          all

             to

Apache	jokes
English	meals
African	cult sermons
American	high schools
Indian	castes
Balinese	widow burnings

. . . .

On Being a Real Person by
Harry Emerson Fostick

———————————————

. . . .

ere's is is sense o distance & confusion

searching of forright clues

they knewgnaw pharoah disguised as

woman disguised as man

eye to brain & right back again

And whan that she hir fader hath yfounde,
Doun on hir knees falleth she to grounde;
Wepynge for tendrenesse in herte blithe,

clear cuts in space & time
& cooking smells time
the smell of time
1 kisten dour ebin 'n eaten frothe

Hi Vicki!

....

cruising   foreign   close

je ne   main streets

regrette

                   blue

                                              nose

can anyone reset   *rien*

. . . .

cruisin

                   blue

                                              rien

omnis scientia bona est

nose shot off in war

day by day we're fallin more. . .

Natures postparadisiac losses A – Z

Trying to cut down /on/

vs digital time

(WAVE DAMN HAM IN AIR)

. . . .

(waving postdigital losses?)

———————————————————————

VE DA

--------------------goose-foot-flesh-step

    (sounds like)

--------------------nature mored

    (same as)

--------------------3 forms of present indicative

    (2nd syllable)

--------------------astral turf

    (1st letter)

--------------------permanent pleats

    (sounds like)

--------------------Buffalo wings

(from such signs whole cultures have been deduced)

(from such sighs even vultures have been seduced)

(dumb luck thighs bring cultures home to roost)

---

items of windhardware still available:

anemometers. generators.
towers. madurai type sailwings.

other alternatives:
lakeside property
the enduring questions

et iam Iunonia laeva parte Samos

simple physics & complex politics of everyday life.

....

"My Commedia" she called it

astride   alight   awash   afoul   agape

orange stuck with cloves or loose necked fowl
(no it wasn't that way at all)

regular rhythm that can collapse a stadium or a bridge

Dr. Heidi's grammar for a nuclear age

....

ia"

awa

loves

eid

Enna Labraid/luad caich,
comarc Bresail/buain blaith.

thickintransigentsmile

   (puddynge)

   (sic) gloria

topological   squeeze   and   stretch

Domiabo damna ustra.   (p.4) DLHR, p.58
                      -charm for sprain-

thick   talk   ers

topological smile

———————————————————

   top   eeze

       lk

poet o the Land-O-Lakes District

     Spitting Imagists

Lord and Lady Elgin and their watches

hard   dry   and   photo   phobic

terrorists burning toast (*boasts?*) in Winnipeg

                        perhaps thi
                           the
                              ing of

---

poet   -O

                    sts?)

We vied to make haste slowly.

You believed there are tears for things.

They wanted the currency of a language reputed

dead.

_____

```
ICARUS F
        F
          F
            F
              F
                A
                  L
                    L
                      I
                        N
                          G
```

Thanks to the students in my August 1987 Language & Thinking workshop at Bard College, who when asked to go out and photograph Icarus falling found him everywhere.

DAEDALUS INTERA (	*et iam Iunonia*	HATING CRETE AND HIS LONG
EXILIUM TACTUSQU	*turning the page*	VE LAND WAS SHUT IN BY THE
CLAUSUS ERAT PELA	*laeva parte Samos*	BLOCK ESCAPE BY LAND AND
OBSTRUAT: ET CAEL	*space becomes time*	HE SAID YET THE SKY IS OPEN
OMNIA POSSIDEAT I	*ightnay to ourningmay*	THOUGH MINOS RULES OVER
DIXIT ET IGNOTAS /	*FAMILY REUNION*	AYING HE SETS HIS MIND AT
NATURAMQUE NOV/	*dark islands up light*	RTS AND CHANGES THE LAWS
A MINIMA COEPTAS]	*appetizers cheese dip*	HE LAYS FEATHERS IN ORDER
UT CLIVO CREVISSE F	*nuts 'n chips dip*	O THAT YOU WOULD THINK
FISTULA DISPARIBUS	*liquid smoke up peps*	SHIONED RUSTIC PANPIPES
TUM LINO MEDIAS E	*up red meat or fowl*	THER. THEN HE FASTENED
ATQUE ITA CONPOSIT	*transector sourire jaune*	H TWINE AND WAX AT THE
VERAS IMITETUR AVE!	*filling a position in space*	CARUS WAS STANDING BY
STABAT ET IGNARUS SI	*was I turning*	ANDLING HIS OWN PERIL
ORE RENIDENTI MODC	*trying to keep*	FUL FACE WOULD NOW
CAPTABAT PLUMAS FLA'	*every moment*	NG BREEZE HAD BLOWN
MOLLIBAT LUSUQUE SU(	*civilization falls every day*	WAX WITH HIS THUMB
IMPEDIEBAT OPUS. POSTC	*behind the words groan*	S FATHER'S WONDROUS
INPOSITA EST GEMINAS O	*esyay onay evitationlay*	G TOUCHES HAD BEEN
IPSE SUUM CORPUS MOTAC	*of every up of or about*	BALANCED HIS BODY
INSTRUIT ET NATUM MEDIC	*fractal prepositions*	RUS FLY THE MIDDLE
ICARE AIT MONEO NE SI DEMI.	*audible in groanwhile*	O LOW THE WATER
GRAVET PENNAS SI CELSIOR IGN	*playing reBach sweet i.e.*	OU GO TOO HIGH
HELICEN IUBEO STRICTUMQUE I	*each second seemed*	WORD OF ORION
INTER UTRUMQUE VOLA.NEC TE 1	*stung my face*	WEEN THE TWO.
ME DUCE CARPE VIAM! PARITER HE	*miles below*	OF FLIGHT AND
TRADIT ET IGNOTAS UMERIS ACCO !	*light coals well*	BOY'S SHOUL

before the cliché becomes real & pan Rupert I'm telling ic sets in father instructs son on rules of flight sky Walker Matt Jack George Ethan Gabe Josh the the fixes strange wings on boys shoulders *laeva parte Samos* not goodbye forever or a suicide note just what's to be expected on every wall on every scrap of paper on every matchbox ALFABETIZACION ES LIBERACION the child becomes a boy the gun becomes the llave key to dedos finger Newton stared too long at the sun (T or F?) Mug Shot 1 Father Fig 2 is this the correct way to address these matters *fuerant Delosque Parosque relictae* you always remember the memory of the person who taught you how to eat artichokes fondly fondly no matter what what inter boy falls out of sky venes and he had said he did only want to show her the

. . . .

calmness of the sea toad not death's German troubled transense dented

dreams of I the I family line Icarus Isaac Iphis Ianthe Io WHAT IS HAS

HAP PENNED BETWEEN you & me to stare so long at pages time turns

granular space feeding flames of at first just the breeze good on tongue 'n

cheek CODE EX MEMO REES first fingers turn to twigs no matter what

has hap end the little boy looks up at skies to which his fathers fingers point

not knowing clouds brief chaotic histories interest us less than *caelum certe*

defacto anon unknown über-object always to prepare them for WARS

BLASTS RAYS VECTORS VALENCES PROCLIVITIES TROPISMS

developing tastes for horror shut in by land'nsea UNDER SOCIAL

CONSTRUCTION I clever one-eyed mechanical monster said

Freud says the family is the greatest enemy of civilization next comes the tribe dead o lust founder of Socrates circular line cool Disco Dans last minute red line blues close thirds nostalgia dear customer in order to show our appreciation meanwhile D hating Crete *dextra Lebinthus erat fecundaque melle Calymne* what you call an he stunted Amercan fertilizer he FreshOffBoat himself told he'd make an ugly girl he say he glad in his long exile bliss on earthe there be at least a Spanish word for snot he think moco longing to see a native land not now Angloterre changed to Anglo Terror 'n right back again before A-OK ☒☑ $$$ cartoon character conversation unit 3 quel est je m'appelle votre nom de plume hating Cretes

. . . .

mythocentric time warped minds separation error 1 clue to: why *Invisible*

Man filed in Sci-fi section malenigma velvet Elvis garish sunsets woman

with undescended voice: body walks off into life leaving her behind

Antheraea polyphemus giant silkworm moth passed from child to child in

kindergarten class the anthropologist observed in his favorite African

tongue shut in by many seasons dry wet dry by the way has anyone seen the

slack lip exercises has any one told the Lord on the hill whats happening in his

kingdom vibrato alphabetizado romantico vatic O many words with tics pop

up pop tart pop art whose genius is to treat zee cheap commoditee with

aggressive rhectorics of glamour over night over you're or my dead your

shoulder you see a flash of light you hear a splash against the law of
redundancy dogs the town one end to end in under yes no Alamagordo she
took her time for the second time but soon she realized it was his time she
was taking blood turned to sap skin to bark the child trapped in her womb
passengers watch your step the child split through the bark the child by five
had called the dog a straddled various Orpheus *frustraque squalidus
dolorque animi lacrimacque alimenta fuere* he said I won't andstay on
eremonycay and sat down in the dream I take my head and go and now
Euridice dying again of what could she complain save she was O to be too

. . . .

beloved to be ludicrous in Berlin start coals now suggested salads: pasta

fruit mixed greens Goldilocks Gadzooks turns out'nup General Delafield on

active duty (he was) only while leading the parade down 5th Ave but surely

the Fred'nGinger'll take this matter it up in only a couch wrecked room

addition backyard barbecue check-point paper plates keep chicken salad

cool til just before Sir Mendel spent his days counting peas Icarus his son

hangs out playing Country 'n Western Civ vol too sky hi sky cap geometries

separate ordure from ardor (chaos) come see the child who sticks his thumb

in yellow wax disappear *deseruitque ducem calique cupidine* hey Freud

suggests monosymbolic form of sons of fathers law of Icarus playing by
Fathers Fig side little knowing the sea would hold him still all these days
still no bitter plaints to gods cruel beyond belief & Bachs fudge organ
exploding in to air out those indoor European roots XXXXXXXXX
Xenophon retreats ten thousand times one of history's great failures takes us
back to Sq.1 Xenophobicalculus Bauhaus build *ing* dung eons o stories sky
hi Xs over Malcolms grandma teaching them how to turn the spoon convex
side up under running water to avoid a splash *melle Calymne* little knowing
tractare pericla melisma telescopes abnormal extension of I's eye adding

. . . .

fixed stars invisible hitherto & other innumerables I warn you of I the heavy

charioteer I when they thought them thin I des invalides I advised by

chickens I confectioneers checkered darkness I mak low skool master sign

waving chicken claw in hemitopical air his fathers fathers send him to the

whine cellar when he misquotes q.e.d.c.f.c.v. his worried father instructs

him in the middle way as Vatican Library seals float for centuries in

Aristotles cloudless blueless skies Libri naturales retinal fluids missa

solemnis splashed in seas pray least Pepys/he bury his/wife w/his cheese in

a Great Fire he say many an a to b to add to the great multitude of attitudes

the great economics of fire obsessed of I I say the sons in the heat of a great
wine *cum puer audaci coepit gaudere volatu* wars the health of the state the
boy rejoicing in bold flight deserts his leader why this desire for open sky
in species w/out wings Tragicus-Logico-Philosophicus jokebox amo amas a
fortune aberrant est meat&potatoes mans hounds tracing scent *tractare
pericla* splash Little Hans Wolf Man's Faster Pussycat Mode of Light fall
in heavy metal tubular razor or we're all amazed at the sight of boys falling
out of for skies haggled spotnick SexPistols' tiny little dots caught in eyes *Is*

. . . .

Excess Hard Times splash quite unnoticed spreading just like the flue

watchout homeboy don't let it catch you and my student says when he gets

bored in Italian class she conjugates the verb scrivere in the future

conditional or he thinks mocomocomoco mother computer aliens calling all

mother gulls and waves recede and islands go dark on the sea s/he Zed have

you noticed that poetry was one of the noble gases ripening the

pomegranate never a cantaloupe or banana then two men have bigfight over

a banana now mega Hertz he dead he can not turn Icarus into the girl Icare

I'carus (*Ikaros*) the classical dictionary says see *Daedalus* (see Perdix) perdiction grammar unit where is I's mother not that she or any other uncommitted 110 amps 15,000 foot extension cord or will you marry a house carpenter and come along with 50 outlets 20 rolls duck tape could save him now bouts too latearly by that I mean by that time they've all come up weeping trees *historia animalium de partibus animalium de generatione animalium* rams butt over column 1 M heavily crowned eagle stuck atop column 2–F in the Nicholas Germanus Almanac a partial solar eclipse *ing* in

. . . .

left margin *ing* in right margin lunar eclipse said he'd be right back in his

sweats carrying blue and red pro sports bag he said on the post-Dodo island

turkeys force-fed the fruit to see if dispersal would resume it DID that was

the flying lesson he couldn't give a flying fuck for less tee-shirt tautologies

& concessions ur distinctions taking place all the time getting better since

you been mine duped *gordius tractus altius egit iter* come a long way

babycakes earths guts 'n all led by the soon to be the i.e. the THE of the

spontaneous generation *RAPIDI VICINIA LOCO SOLIS* for one breath o

ODORATAS SOLIDO CATULLUS in DC THE Red Sea is THE EthiOpian restaurant IRON IC ICON IC ION IC 'N ALL kickback systems Oral stimulus bOund WHAT will keep us alOft in the systematic tic yOu tOck eat drink tOO much O vidius decried what did SapphO teach but HOW TO lOve Other girls 'n Other *tristia* tOpiques tOpi low cal SHOWDOWN EXTREMIST EXPLOSION TARGETS BLOCKADE SANCTIONS WAR BOMBS HIJACK WAR HATE CRIMES RACE FUNDAMENTALLISTS

. . . .

HIJACK THEORISTS hi Jack! a child who decided to name himself after

his favorite cheese he asked OK DAD what's really the difference between

the Buddha and the Statue of Liberty *Icare dixit ubi es pater noster*

fisherman shepherd treeman plowman woman spies them too and they do

stand stupefied believing them to be gods that they can fly through thin air

keeping fit father 'n son alike he cried *father* and the dark water took its

name from his 2) bend knees head forward round back stretch right arm out

right side lower arm raise arm bend knees repeat with left arm his son
Icarus stood by and little knowing he was handling his own perilous argot
got it right HOW TO your French German English accent before you hit
the road *puer Icarus una furtiva lacrima stabat et ignarus sua se tractare
pericla* or perils of English history in rhyme fairhaired Saxons came and
kindred Angles found a home to which they gave a name instructing in the
fatal art of flight fair Lebinthus on the right now his dogs bark down the

. . . .

night never let him out of sight kissed his sons 'n let them go first date fig 3

or 4 Post Correct AC to still the turbulent air voracious wind storms flaming

hard rock suns to still think still ideals still ought in still fallen words

worlds leave the still rime behind to marinate overnight coals glowing no

flames shooting into insubstantial air *ubo roi es* erstwhile ergonomic lads of

teachable minds sons O Pierot perfecting arts o war the father digs the grave

the mother *garrula luminoso perdix* a um perched for a word or 3) perfect palmer his sweet penisship de scribed on de texticular nite you did not withhold your son from me bless you Abe babe or Malcolm ex-ladies man nights they serve baked beans 'n fries modesta peduncle punch errasty Hells Proverbs live from hell EXTERIOR WASH WAX WAYNE ENTER RIGHT EXIT LEFT THANK YOU HAVE A NICE stamp out fires with Morris dances bird he soar too high he soar on his own wingding laws dis courage to think of other order exorcise the male the sport of archery as

. . . .

Zeno's arrows fly in no time to combine pleasure with necessity during the

burial a noisy partridge all newcomer to the ranks of birds to fallen words

worlds just beginning poofs all over grieving fathers HEY ICKY PLEASE

DON'T BANG THE SCREEN DOOR WHEN YOU LEAVE! or parting

same as nothing to do nothing to do stick some mustard in your shoe

SUFFER *ing* up & about from over & out to Mussolini Afraido parallel

parking unit 4) furtiva lacrimosa mother ain't no other mother here bouts or

Mussolini said a bomb exploding in the desert is like a rose bursting into bloom is like a pull toy pull string is like a is like a is like amusia auto phagia a tresia a stenosis o the luminous ass an as if pulled by a string lips purse resembling anus in or of certain iconographies of desire i.e. eggs ovoid for good REASON she REASON subscribe now get 1 free she avoid

. . . .

pregnancy strange bird and the sun softened the fragrant wax beesleaving

dotted lines in the not insubstantial air of *ad pater infelix nec iam pater*

Icare dixit Icare dixit ubi es qua te regione requium Icare dicebat and the grief

remains buried in the obscurity of the Latin that bears the names of the

bewreathed no maters buoyant warm cracks in wings floating on dark water chance selects for natures never seen before seen in this form perhaps garrulous perdition sucked all outlets dry crowded house goes dark flamable dispathetic Roman tic *nihil est* how to: have hi-flyin ideas under fallen yellow arches could be another U-HAUL adventure in family moving fitness 'n fun under certain words transmitting acquired characteristics

. . . .

TOLL ½ MILE AHEAD downwords roads punctuated evolution now then

redundancies laws of nature kill USALLINTHEENDUPADNAUSEAM in

sidewalk cafés A-OK how *did* Socrates save Xenophon in that crackling

ancient air MOVEITYOURSELFASSHOLE baby's head appears pig runs

out from under bed the only time she went on Dr. Father's rural housecalls house calls a name that needn't but could be Emma she knewknows large flat surfaces tend to warp she saw a flash of light in the sky just as she turned away and he cursing his own skill nay take then courage to banish from your heart hopeless love arms were bare as he beat them up and down

. . . .

but lacking wings Palestrami composed the Missa Papae Marcelli to

convince 'M not to ban polyphony Missa Massa Major Mozart a um und

gentle complex music making plants grow twice as big as 2nd thoughts

flying low and threatening dark clouds over maps in keys of asia minor

Ovid said his mind was bent to tell of bodies changed to new forms O Jude
don't be too long in 2nd story allegories Da Vinci faults the butterfly for
mistaking hot wax for suns of fallen rock star zones fallen stone crater lakes

. . . .

springs up no hope but Hobbes levitation hope for Pig Latinate Orackle

& O the skysonsclamor for fathersnamesalbino & Isaac's Falls & Abe's

garrulousstrangebirdmothers & Iphis nottheboy she wished to be in Bk. IX

what if when *we* died *our* feet stuck up in the air like pigs in the mud on the
moon Pleiades 'n you are set 'n I lie like a rug alone with the father wanting
a son dressed like theboysheneverwas identified in the translation as fair

. . . .

Ianthes lover ready to die for theher thefamily thetribe therace thenation

thelaw the onthemoney big idea natures surrogatetail won't tell how or why

or why native Pig Latin speakers do not come plain that thegods are cruel

NO not even if Daedelus returned on butchersbeeswaxwings and Icarus in a variant translation pilots WWI onto Marerotic fields free dixie cup dispensers 'n *lacrimae sunt verba secutae* ist it killed the Romans now its

. . . .

killing   me   to   mock   those   who   choose

to   believe   what   they   believe   only   in   the   form   of

poetry attachées de la cire ...... Mais rsvps regretted physed physy Ed's ed

past tense ediddling with many fates ewhiche in fact to you who but lately
were   a   girl   are   now   a   boy   and   Iphis   theorized
Ovidious refundulating Ibid to Ibis strange sweet garrulous bird of she the

. . . .

I lines Io Ianthe Isis Icarus Isaac Iachhus Idalia Iphigenia crossing in their

flagrant saffron mantles breeze of more transvestments & vestigian tables

dan dey dreadmed could cause the splash to splash again against the the

splashes *guerrilla luminoso* nocount Latins less Gks but gt new restaurant
opening ethnic digital war on forehead of Zeus too numorose to not suspend

. . . .

the now substantial aer-O-mythologeewhiz gone sour or sore soar to sorrow

plausit   pennis   testataque   guadia   cantu   est   over   UNDER

STANDABOUT not recognizing who or what they were or who we are

. . . .

just trying on the sadness of the verb to be we hope is not too fffffallen to

. . . .

fall over

JOURNAL OF A LUNAR ECLIPSE

we forget . . . . in order to pass from one word to the next

PHASE ONE

let's not meet again by accident

(she dreams she's in a French horror movie)

postcards from the French revolution:

waving from hot-air balloon

top-O-the 18th century

all classes of people ergo sum

all those familiar faces ad hominem

sidereal messenger

waving back from below

PHASE TWO

let's dream pizza French hot waving

taboos returning oops return to zero

—which when followed as strictly as savages—

now count backwards zero return minus additives

this experience of madness extremely coherent:

oops have we skipped number # 4

let's write oops opera while modicum est patria

this engine don't sound like it's gonna

to # 5: kingdom phylum class order family genus

species on the harmonica

or mnemonic # 6: kingsplaychessonfiberglassstools, etc.

(they told us to please get off the mnemonic)

PHASE THREE

woodchuck   *pickle*   *desperate*   *zygote*   *mnemonic*

faith healing   *gimlet*   *olivetti*

(how sad Scarlatti ((A?, D?)) got too fat to play)

PHASE FOUR

taboo   *return*   *oops*   *zero*   *Queendom*   *mnemonic*   *engine*

    species   *think*   *fat*

          return   *pickle*

I liked it when he asked which side of the mirror are you on

[Significance of basic color triad among the Ndembu: milk and semen, blood and earth, shit and death. We like to think that we think we've gotten a bit further than that.]

PHASE FIVE

Salut Mirielle, comment ça va? Es tu malade?

the much neglected fact

hitherto unnoticed

in fact overlooked

in fact much ignored

in fact misunderstood

I have discovered

I will not belabor

(a man runs in to tell me I'm double parked / theme of the

resurrection, etc.)

PHASE SIX

salut hitherto urgent lotus mnemonic siren pod errata

further than that Hobbes thought there were passions peculiar to every class:
aristocratic pride, bourgeois desire for power, working class desire for revenge (did he
mention this?), bourgeois pride,
aristocratic fear of revenge

PHASE SEVEN

play the record at slow speed and wear red-chequered pants

what drives us is fear, desire, and electrical impulse (same thing?)

(she taught for instance me or her all I or she think I or we or they need to know about OLIVES us and them as well as how to)

fear of desire

fear of squinting

desire to suddenly arise and:

LOOK AROUND

——were I to choose an auspicious image for the new millennium——

_____

_____

_____

_____

Calvino   *albino*   *o love*   *continental*   *permutation*

desire to fear and

desire at precisely 9:20 pm

mnemonic

    mnemonic

      albino

        desire

_____*permutation*

                red-chequered

                    silent

                        pod

                          erratum

AMERRATA

TV MANAGUA   dog   barks   then   howls   you

weren't   asked   to   share   she   says   the

one   about   the   goat   is   my   story

margin   to   margin   it's   the   marginaise

the   moon   describes   the   stream   he

wrote   stream   pumping   through   glade   Om

I   nous   scene   of   another   early   morning

body   dump   there   are   no   seasons   on

TV   or   Sandino's   last   supper

strange   as   it   may   seem   you   are

standing   before   a   firing   squad   basic

skills   improved   high   degree   of   literacy

does   the   the   mind   play   with

an   idea   it's   a   it's   a

        of   the   idea   of   déjà   vu

Foner says Latin America has been the story

of trying to sustain revolution and that's

our story too which revenge is

the revenge of the real or destinies

74

left   or   right   turns   into   lowgrade   practical   joke   truth

false   backfires   outside   window   sound   of

no   truck   with   one   shot   trick   cigar   pop

goes   another   weasel   *agonia*   nachos   sunset

----

the preceding is a sense perception induced by light   entering   the   eye

AUTOBIOGRAPHIALITTERARIA I

for Tina Darragh

worn extravagance is yes
and under blue dodge all

but then first famous
            Celtic bell
        the general
some where cow crow

                                        and lips aping

and Jane

despite Wallace lies

            did

jelly/male/guilty/pride

she   prehistoric

stocking   bolts

growlight

wretched   tine

    peace be

    photon

    twist

    cork aground

butter ageless

thin / chair / upset

blue ford or toggle bolt

3rd peek sea lab to betray

under cake excell

child and quark

mute   film

water   aquiline

land gauge open day

roll elude

to hear

thunder / mylar / grown

to see

blues all gone and enter

Canal Street pie

voices dome the too

genre / dark / fiction / crack

blue d'ark and el

heare laughteare quite thicke

mother oughten / err / to goodknot

named / blameless / sky

toward never struck

I   cousin   cousin   floating

there   omnivorous

there   in wading let

station

dark

under

cry

/the/falls

long / blues / clot

arc & broke

pees

mem-O-rees

coastal jar

ancient stew

department orge

  light pulls bleached to gut

   oh us!

                                                              skin a grand

                                    librarians

Pelham   stomp   Georgia   lay

grass   waist

the   dense   engine   irretrievable

the   lake   joy   itself

                kite / drained / planet

their no English being was.   anon.

black into color

brittle/mud/dreams/burned

me/ghost/portable

                         color into black

                                     burned/dreams/mud/brittle

                                     /portable/

coal   dark   oboe

3rd   ave

over   anon

light / dark / skate

which no is yes

AUTOBIOGRAPHIALITTERARIA II

for Holly Swain

:MYSTORY:WHATS WRONG WITH THIS PICTURE:

:BEFORE: :THEN:

V.WOOLF.J.JOYCE.JELLY.ROLL.MORTON.HE.DEAD.I.HAVE.WANT

ED.TO.HAVE.THE.DRIVE.TO.KNÖW.MY.OWN.STORY.THERE.BY.

TOUCHING.THE.VIOLENCE.IN.THE.MECHANISM.ITSELF.ONLY.TO.

BE.REPLACED.WITH.ALL.AND.THEN.AND.WHERE.ALONG.THE.WA

Y.IT.[EIS].BIFURCATES.ÖEISÒ.**FROST**.IN.OLD.GERMAN.**PASSION**.

IN.GREEK.AND.LATIN.THEN.THE.FATHTHER.WAS.ARRESTED.IN.G

ERMANY.ON.THE.EVE.OF.ANOTHER.WAR.THEN.HE.SAID.HE.WAS.

THERE.TO.STUDY.THE.GERMAN.LANGUAGE.MUSIC.AND.ENGINE

:MYSTORY:WHATS WRONG WITH THIS PICTURE:

:BEFORE: :THEN:

ERING.THEY.COULD.NOT.BELIEVE.THE.COINCIDENCE.FACTS.AR
E.OK.HE.SAID.THEY.ARE.BETTER.THAN.LOOKING.IN.THE.MIRROR.
SEE.HOW.THE.AIR.IS.FULL.OF.AIR.A.NOTE.S.O.S.NOT.GEOMETRY.
OF.THE.EMOTIONS.MOTHER.SPOKE.SPANISH.AND.ENGLISH.AS.A.
CHILD.SHE.WAS.TEASED.BECAUSE.SHE.SAID.LOOKING-GLASS.IN
STEAD.OF.MIRROR.IS.THIS.A.PICTURE.OF.A.FACT.THE.LENS.GIVE
S.ON.A.CLEAR.BLUE.YELLOW.GREEN.MOMENT.THEN.NEI.ÖNEIÒ.
TO.BE.EXCITED.TO.SHINE.TO.LEAD.ALSO.NEIGW.ÖNEIGWÒ.OF.RI
VERS.WATERS.WASHING.THE.FATHTHER.HIMSELF.PLAYING.PIAN

96

:MYSTORY:WHATS WRONG WITH THIS PICTURE:

:BEFORE: :THEN:

O.FOR.SILENT.ÜjÜî.MOVIES.[DONTWORRYSAYSTHEDYINGMANI'V
EHADAGOOD86YEARSBUTDADSAYSHISDAUGHTERYOUAREONLY76]
IT.I.WANT.TO.SAY.FOLLOWS.THEN.THAT.SHOULD.BE.THE.NEXT.WO
RD.IS.IT.WORTH.USURING.METAPHOR.TO.SAY.THE.MAN.WHO.SOLD.
CANDY.AT.THE.CORNER.STORE.HAD.A.FACE.AS.OPEN.AS.A.SHUCK
ED.OYSTER.[CHILDHOODISFULLOFHORROR].MUCH.LATER.THE.DAU
GHTER.FOUND.OUT.THE.FATHTHER.HAD.NAMED.A.LOW.LEVEL.TRA
NSMITTER.AFTER.HER.DURING.ANOTHER.WAR.THE.GERMAN.ROOT.

:MYSTORY:WHATS WRONG WITH THIS PICTURE:

:BEFORE: :THEN:

WAS.**FROST**.FINALLY.INTELLIGENCE.GOT.OUT.AND.THE.WE.WO
N.THE.WAR.THEN.THERE.IS.THE.THING.IS.PLAYING.AT.THE.MOV
IES.THE.SILENT.ROOTS.OF.A.LANGUAGE.ARE.CHEMICAL.ELEME
NTS.BOPP.FOLLOWING.SANSKRIT.GRAMMARIANS.THOUGHT.TH
EY.WERE.ALL.MONOSYLLABIC.THEN.THERE.ARE.THE.STRETCH-
GRADE.VOWELS.YES.YES.I.LEARNED.ALL.THESE.THINGS.AT.THE.
SO.TO.SPEAK.KNEES.OF.MY.SPANISH.MOTHER.MY.CORNISH.FA
THTHER.MY.RUSSIAN.UNCLE.&.INTERNATIONALISTA.COMMUN

:MYSTORY:WHATS WRONG WITH THIS PICTURE:

:BEFORE: :THEN:

IST.AUNT.MY.ENGLISH.GRANDMOTHER.[THEREMAYHAVEBEENA

MOORTOO].EX.LIBRIS.CUBA.LIBRA.ONE.DAY.SHE.THREW.HER.LU

NCH.AWAY.AND.CARRIED.THE.GARBAGE.TO.WORK.[THISISANOL

DFAMILYSTORY].THINKING.OF.GREEK.MYTHS.SPANISH.TRAGED

IES.ITALIAN.OPERAS.ÖGULLÒ.ÖÒ.ÖDOLMENÒ.ÖMENHIRÒ.THE.O

NLY.CORNISH.WORDS.CITED.AS.SURVIVING.MODERN.ENGLISH.

AND.THE.LAST.TWO.JUST.BARELY.BARLEY.THE.ONLY.CELTS.WH

O.LOST.THEIR.TONGUE.DOES.THIS.ALARM.YOU.HE.ASKED.ME.[N

:MYSTORY:WHATS WRONG WITH THIS PICTURE:

:BEFORE: :THEN:

OCAUSEFORVIOLENCEORWARSHETHOUGHTINSILENCE].ÜjÜî.SO
METHING.ABOUT.A.CORNISH.LASH.FILLING.UP.ON.SUCCOTASH.TH
EN.LATER.MOTHER.CONFESSED.SHE.NEVER.LIKED.LIVER.AND.SHE.
DIDN'T.BELIEVE.IN.GOD.DID.SHE.SAY.THE.HIDDEN.FAT.OR.FACT.OF
DOUBT.HER. *TOPIARY. GAZE.*HER. *CONVEX. VOCABULARIES.*HER.CONCA
VE.SMILE.[YOUDON'TPERSUADESOMEONETOSMILE].THE.CHILD.CO
MES.BRINGING.SOUND.AND.LIGHT.THERE.ARE.A.LOT.OF.ÖSHEÒS.IN.
THIS.STORY.ÖSHEÒ.WANTS.TO.PERFECT.THE.GRAPPLING.ARTS.ÖSH

100

:MYSTORY:WHATS WRONG WITH THIS PICTURE:

:BEFORE: :THEN:

EÒ.SAY.SHE.WANTS.SPIRITUALITY.TO.CHANGE.THE.DIRECTION.OF.
HER.POWER.ÖSHEÒ.ÖSHEÒ.SAY.ALL.THESE.THINGS.ARE.THE.THIN
GS.THAT.I.TRULY.LOVE.IN.THE.MS.OF.THE.FIFTEENTH.CENTURY.M
ISSA.NOTES.BLEED.THROUGH.FROM.THE.OTHER.SIDE.OF.THE.PAGE.
FILLING.IN.BLANKS.ON.THE.STAVES.AND.COMPLICATING.THE.MU
SIC.

SELECTED SOURCES

John Cage, *For the Birds*, Marion Boyars, Boston, 1981.
Geoffrey Chaucer, *Canterbury Tales*, ed. A.C. Cawley, Dutton, New York, 1966.
Mrs. Charles H. Gardner, *English History in Rhyme*, Walker, Evans & Cogswell, Charleston, S.C., 1959.
Jessica Grim, *Locale*, Potes & Poets, 1994.
Leonardo da Vinci, *Notebooks, Vol. II*, ed. Jean Paul Richter, Dover, New York, 1970.
Ovid, *Metamorphoses*, Vols. I & II, Books VIII, IX, X. English trans. Frank Justus Miller, Harvard University Press, Cambridge, 1958.
Plato, "Euthyphro," *The Collected Dialogues*, ed. Edith Hamilton & Huntington Cairns, Bollingen Series LXXI, Pantheon, New York, 1961.
Sappho, *Lyrics in the Original Greek*, with trans. by Willis Barnstone, Anchor Books, New York, 1965.
Lilly C. Stone, *English Sports and Recreations*, University of Virginia Press, Charlottesville, 1974.
Genre Tallique, *Glances*, Pre-Post-Eros Editions, G.V., P.E., frothcoming [?], 2000+.
James Travis, *Early Celtic Versecraft*, Cornell University Press, Ithaca, 1973.
Vatican Library Book and Manuscript Collection, *Rome Reborn: The Vatican Library and Renaissance Culture*, Library of Congress, Washington, D.C., Jan.8–April 30, 1993.
Rosmarie Waldrop, *The Hunky of Pippin's Daughter* (cover blurb), Station Hill, Barrytown, N.Y., 1986.
Victor Weisskopff, telephone conversation.

UNIVERSITY PRESS OF NEW ENGLAND publishes books under its own imprint and is the publisher for Brandeis University Press, Brown University Press, Dartmouth College, Middlebury College Press, University of New Hampshire, University of Rhode Island, Tufts University, University of Vermont, Wesleyan University Press, and Salzburg Seminar.

JOAN RETALLACK is currently on the faculty of the interdisciplinary University Honors Program at the University of Maryland and is an associate of the Institute for Writing and Thinking at Bard College. In 1993–94 she was Visiting Butler Chair Professor of English in the Poetics Program at the State University of New York at Buffalo. In addition to her poetry she has published numerous critical essays on historical and philosophical traditions of the contemporary avant-garde, writing extensively on the work of John Cage. Her most recent book of poetry, *Errata 5uite* (Edge Books) won the 1994 Columbia Book Award, judged by Robert Creeley.

Library of Congress Cataloging-in-Publication Data
Retallack, Joan.
   A F T E R R I M A G E S / Joan Retallack.
     p.   cm. — (Wesleyan poetry)
   ISBN 0–8195–2219–8 (cl). — ISBN 0–8195–1223–0 (pa)
    I. Title.   II. Title: AFTERRIMAGES.   III. Series.
   PS3568.E76A67   1995
   811'.54—dc20   94–48727
   ∞

Lightning Source UK Ltd.
Milton Keynes UK
UKHW01f1941260618

324833UK00001B/85/P